Thanksgiving crafts and cookbook /
J 745.5 HAT   220759

Hathaway, Nancy,

OCT 18 82	OCT	
OCT 11 '83	NOV 03	
OCT 11 '84		
OCT 16 85		
OCT 14 86		
OCT 13 '87		
OCT 13 '88		
OCT 12		
OCT 11 '90		

CAT. NO 24 162   PRINTED IN U.S.A.   BRODART

J 745.5   1557
HATHAWAY, NANCY
Thanksgiving Crafts & Cookbook

LONGLAC PUBLIC LIBRARY

THANKSGIVING
CRAFTS AND COOKBOOK

LONGLAC PUBLIC LIBRARY

THANKSGIVING
CRAFTS and COOKBOOK

BY NANCY HATHAWAY

With Illustrations By Hannah Berman

HARVEY HOUSE • NEW YORK

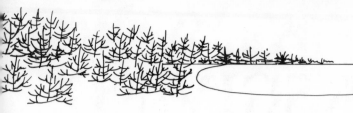

Text Copyright ©1979 by Nancy Hathaway
Illustrations Copyright ©1979 by Hannah Berman

All rights reserved, including
the right to reproduce this book
or portions thereof in any form.

Manufactured in the United States of America
ISBN 0-8178-6110-6
Library of Congress Card Catalogue No. 78-73829

Harvey House, Publishers
20 Waterside Plaza, New York, New York 10010
Published in Canada by Fitzhenry & Whiteside, Ltd., Toronto

Table of Contents

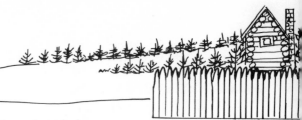

The First Thanksgiving

The winter of 1620 was long and hard. Earlier that year, the Pilgrims from England had landed in the New World at a place they named *Plymouth* in what would become the state of Massachusetts. By the time the winter was over, all of the Pilgrims had gone hungry and half had died of illness. As they planted their crops in the spring of 1621, many of the survivors worried that their journey to America would end in disaster.

But the harvest was good. The Pilgrims made friends with the native Indians, who gave them seeds for corn and taught them many things about life in the New World. By harvest time the Pilgrims knew they could survive.

In the fall of 1621, after the hard work of bringing in the crops and before winter's cold, the Pilgrims decided to give thanks and celebrate. They invited the Indian Chief Massasoit and his tribe to join them for a feast. The Pilgrims shot wild turkeys and ducks. The Indians brought five deer. Together they cooked the meat and prepared cornbread, baked roots, steamed clams, smoked eels, peas and salad greens. They drank wine made from wild grapes.

The festival was held beside a brook and lasted three days. When the people weren't eating, they danced and played games and shot targets with bows and arrows or muskets. Afterward, the friendship between Pilgrim and Indian had grown — as had their stomachs — and the Pilgrims were ready for winter.

Today, we still celebrate Thanksgiving, in the United States on the fourth Thursday in November and in Canada on the second Monday in October. It is a time of fun and good food, and it is also a time to remind ourselves of all that we have to be thankful for — the people who love us, the things we like to do, the beauty of our world.

CRAFTS

Thanksgiving Collage

The most important thing we can do at Thanksgiving time — even more important than eating! — is to remember everything we have to be thankful for. A good way to do this is to make a Thanksgiving collage. A collage is a collection of pictures, drawings, scraps of paper and small objects arranged to make one big picture. Almost anything can go into a collage, as long as you can glue it down on the paper. Your collage will be a reminder of your personal Thanksgiving. And it will be completely original.

LONGLAC PUBLIC LIBRARY

WHAT YOU NEED

one large sheet construction paper or cardboard
pictures of things you are thankful for: photographs of
     your family, pictures cut from magazines, small
     pictures you paint or draw yourself
any of these: scraps of colored paper, wrapping paper,
     tissue paper, silver foil, material, greeting cards,
     yarn, crayons, paints, felt-tip pens, leaves, buttons,
     labels
scissors
white glue or rubber cement

WHAT TO DO

Collect as many small pictures or items as you can find or make. Don't forget to put in pictures of everyone in your family. You might also add pictures of your pets, a favorite teacher, your friends, your home, a hobby you enjoy, your favorite sports or musical instruments, a place you like and so on.

Arrange these pictures on a large piece of construction paper or cardboard. For extra color, add bits of colored paper, wrapping paper, foil or anything else you think might look good.

Glue everything down. Collages usually look better if you overlap the pictures a little bit. Some pictures can be right side up, some can be sideways and some can be

14

upside down. Use your imagination to come up with an interesting design.

Add any final touches you think would improve your composition. You might want to paste down a tiny twig (maybe from a special tree) or add a dab of bright-colored paint.

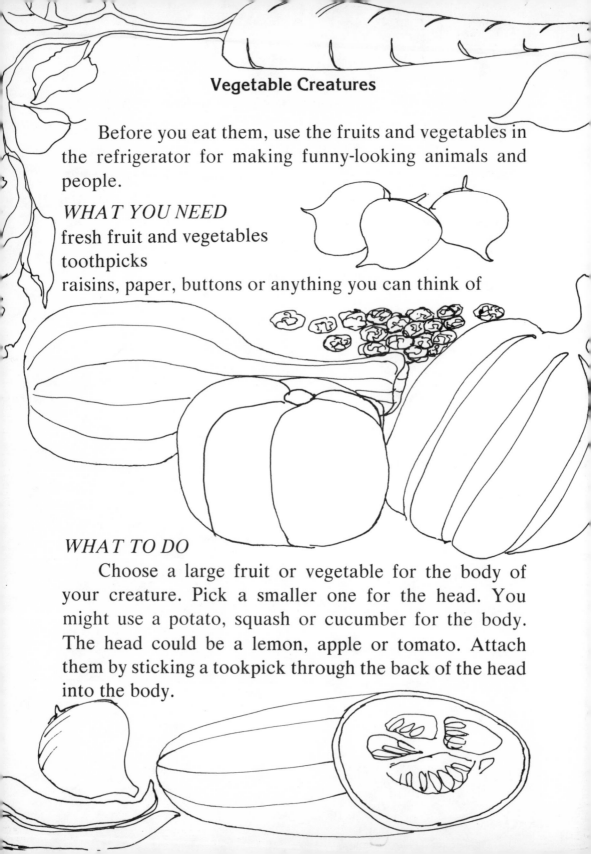

Vegetable Creatures

Before you eat them, use the fruits and vegetables in the refrigerator for making funny-looking animals and people.

WHAT YOU NEED
fresh fruit and vegetables
toothpicks
raisins, paper, buttons or anything you can think of

WHAT TO DO
Choose a large fruit or vegetable for the body of your creature. Pick a smaller one for the head. You might use a potato, squash or cucumber for the body. The head could be a lemon, apple or tomato. Attach them by sticking a tookpick through the back of the head into the body.

Now use your imagination. Toothpicks can be arms or legs. Beans and small peppers make good arms too — or ears, or even hair. Raisins or buttons, attached with toothpicks, can be eyes. And you can always draw a face on paper and stick it on with toothpicks.

After you have finished your vegetable creatures, let everyone admire them for a while. You might even want to take a picture of them, because they will not keep. You might as well eat them!

Paper Bag Puppets

Paper bag puppets are easy to make and fun to use. For Thanksgiving, try making Pilgrims, Indians or even a turkey. Then, you can perform your own puppet shows.

WHAT YOU NEED
small brown paper bags
poster paints and brushes
scissors
pencil
white glue
any of these: beads, feathers, buttons, fluffy white cotton,
    material scraps, colored paper

18

WHAT TO DO

Using a pencil, draw on the paper bag the rough outlines of the puppet. On one side of the bag, draw the front of the puppet. On the other side, draw the back. If the bag is the kind that also has sides, remember to draw the sides of the puppet. You can do this by making sure that the shoulders in front are connected to the shoulders in the back, that hair is drawn on the sides of the bag, and that any special details, like belts or hairbands, go all the way around the bag. If the bag has only two sides, it will be easier.

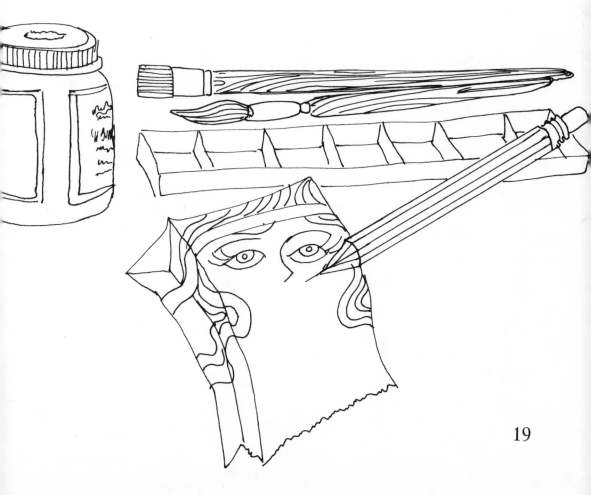

19

Paint the design. The hair will probably cover all four sides of the bag plus the entire top. It is easier if you paint the hair last.

When the paint is dry, add details. For example, you could glue on small buttons, beads or paper feathers. White cotton can be an old man's beard. Colored paper can be an Indian vest with fringe, a Pilgrim's apron or a belt bucket.

When everything is dry, try the puppet on your hand. If your hands are big enough, cut a small square on each side of the bag. Put your thumb through one hole and your little finger through the other. Now your puppet has arms.

Pilgrim and Indian Eggs

Egg people are a little pudgy around the middle and some of them are completely empty-headed. But they're a lot more interesting than Easter eggs and just as much fun to make. Paint them as Indians or Pilgrims and use them for a Thanksgiving display.

WHAT YOU NEED

eggs
poster paints and brushes
a cardboard cylinder from inside a roll of toilet paper
construction paper or light cardboard
white glue
scissors
pencil

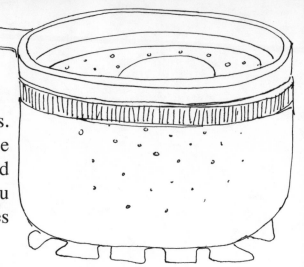

WHAT TO DO

First, prepare the eggs. One way to do this is to make hardboiled eggs. You should ask a grown-up to show you how to do this since it takes boiling hot water.

Another way is to make a hole in the shell and simply shake the egg out of it. Make a hole in the round end of the egg. Use the tip of the scissors. The hole should be no larger than a dime. Hold the egg carefully over a bowl. Begin to shake it. Soon the egg will start dribbling out into the bowl. First the white will come out, then the yolk. When the shell is empty, rinse it out with water and set it aside for a few minutes to dry.

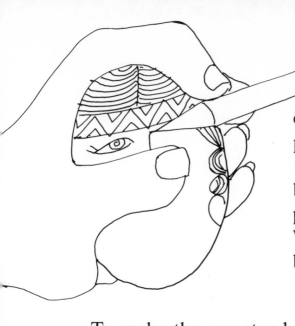

Draw a face and simple clothing on the egg. Then paint the top half of the egg — the face, hair, hat or headband. Set it down to dry, perhaps inside the egg carton. When it is dry, paint the bottom half.

To make the egg stand up, cut a pair of shoes out of light cardboard or construction paper. The shoes should be about this size and shape:

Glue the bottom of the egg (where the hole is) to the shoes. Make sure it is balanced. The egg will stand up. This method works well with hollow eggs.

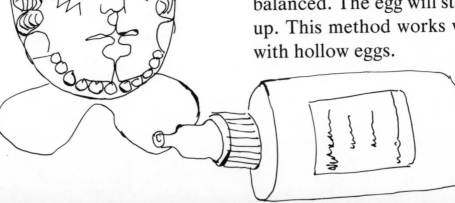

With either hardboiled or hollow eggs, try this: cut a small section from the cardboard cylinder. Paint it the same color as the bottom of the egg. Then simply set the egg inside the cylinder. The cylinder will look like clothing, and the egg will not tip over.

Decorate the eggs with small paper feathers or with Pilgrim hats. You can glue paper arms to the sides if you want. To make a hat, cut a circle out of colored paper about this size and shape:

Place it carefully over the Pilgrim's head. It will form the brim of a hat. Paint everything above the circle the same color as the brim. Your Pilgrim eggs will look like they are wearing hats.

Patchwork Placemats

Patchwork reminds us of earlier times when people saved each scrap and made something beautiful and useful from it. You can do the same thing by using paper and material scraps to make patchwork placemats.

WHAT YOU NEED

12'' x 18'' construction paper
scraps of material and colored paper
white glue or rubber cement
a ruler
a pencil
scissors

WHAT TO DO

Choose a sheet of construction paper in a color you do *not* want to use. Draw a patchwork pattern on the paper. Simple patterns can be made of repeated triangle and square shapes. Other patchwork patterns use stars or repeated flower designs. Make any kind of design you want. You may want to use a ruler. When the design is finished, cut out the patches and use them as patterns.

Take a sheet of paper in a color you *do* want to use. This will be the background. To make patches, take one of the patterns you have already cut out. Trace around the outline with a pencil and cut along the pencil line. Cut patches from a variety of paper and material and glue to the background.

You can also make patchwork placemats with no pattern at all. Cut the patches in any shapes you can think of. Paste them right down on the paper. The design does not have to be neat or even. In the old days, people called this design "crazy quilt." Use as many kinds of paper and material as you can find. Glue them down carefully. You will have a beautiful set of crazy placemats.

Walnut Mayflower Placecards

The Pilgrims sailed to Plymouth in a small wooden ship called the Mayflower. With walnuts and toothpicks, you can make tiny Mayflowers and use them as Thanksgiving placecards.

WHAT YOU NEED

walnuts
toothpicks
colored paper

modeling clay
felt-tip pens
scissors

WHAT TO DO

Carefully crack the walnuts so they break into two equal halves. Remove the nut and the hard membranes inside. The shell will be the hull of the ship.

Next, make the sail. Use light-weight colored paper. Or, use plain white paper and paint it. Cut the paper in a square shape a little larger than the walnut. On each square, write the name of someone who will be at your party. With a toothpick or the sharp end of a scissors, make a very small hole in the upper and lower edges of the paper. Insert the toothpick into these tiny holes so that the paper bulges out. The toothpick is now the mast, and the paper is the sail, billowing out as though it were filled with wind.

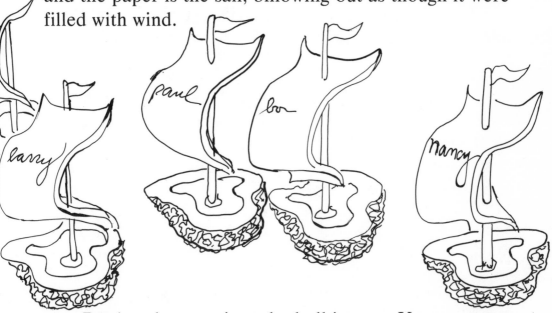

Putting the mast into the hull is easy. You can even put more than one mast in each ship. Just take a small ball of modeling clay. Press it into the bottom of the hull. Stick the toothpick, with the sail attached, into the clay. Your Mayflower placecard is complete.

Plymouth Village Diorama

Using only everyday materials, you can make a miniature Plymouth Village — all inside a cardboard box.

WHAT YOU NEED

a cardboard box
poster paints and brushes
construction paper

tape
white glue
scissors

WHAT TO DO

A diorama is a scene enclosed in a setting — like a box. To make one, choose a box with a missing side. Tissue boxes or shoe boxes are especially good. Paint the background inside the box. You might paint mountains, a few trees and sky. Don't forget to paint the top and bottom of the inside of the box.

Now paint or draw the things you want to put inside the box. Make some trees out of brown and green paper. Or paint some trees with orange, red and yellow leaves — the colors of fall. You might want some cut-outs of people, ships or animals. Or make a Thanksgiving feast table.

Pilgrim huts and Indian teepees are a good addition. To make a teepee, first cut out a half circle of paper. Decorate it. Fold it into a cone and tape it together. Cut a small opening for a door. For a Pilgrim cabin, find a small paper box. Cut out windows and doors. Don't forget the chimney.

When all the pieces for the diorama are finished, cut some thin strips of heavy paper. Fold them into triangles like this:

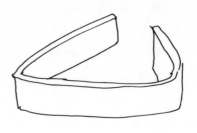

Tape the two ends together. Glue or tape part of the triangle to the figure like this:

Then, paste or tape the bottom of the triangle to the floor of the box. The figure will stand.

For extra touches, find some small twigs. Inside the diorama, they will look like trees or logs. Add pebbles for rocks. Or make small animals out of modeling clay.

If you like making dioramas, try making a city scene, a scene from the Middle Ages with a castle, a prehistoric forest with plastic dinosaurs or a room of a house — perhaps the kitchen on Thanksgiving day.

Harvest Wall Hanging

The Harvest Wall Hanging is a long piece of material decorated with paper fruits and vegetables — some real and some made-up. Hang it on a kitchen wall. The bigger and more colorful you make it, the more dramatic it is.

WHAT YOU NEED

construction paper
scraps of material
white glue
a piece of solid-color
    material at least a yard
    long
needle and thread
a straight stick
pencil
scissors

33

LONGLAC PUBLIC LIBRARY

WHAT TO DO

Draw simple fruits and vegetables on brightly colored paper. Make your designs big. Glue on leaves. Use any colors you want. Red apples and green peppers are nice — but so are blue beets and purple pears.

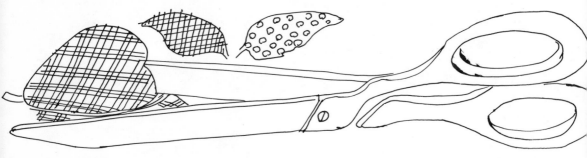

For variety, make a few fruits or vegetables from printed cloth. First, glue a piece of material to construction paper. When the glue is dry, you will be able to cut the material just like paper. Use it to make checked bananas, a flowered eggplant or striped carrots.

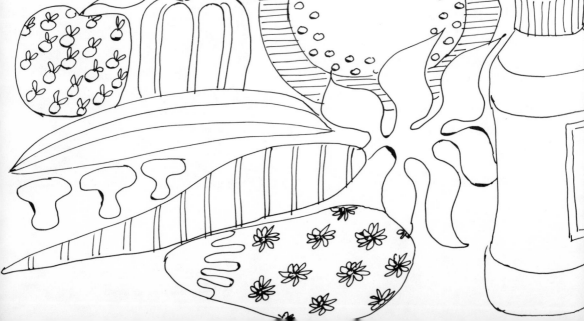

When you have finished a large group of fruits and vegetables, cut the piece of plain material. It should be at least a yard long (or even longer). The width of the material depends upon the stick you are using. You could use a ruler, a long wooden spoon, a chopstick or a branch from a tree. Cut the material so its width is a little narrower than the stick.

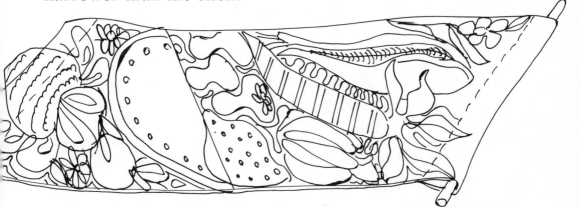

With the needle and thread, make a wide hem at the top of the material. Later, you will put the stick through this hem.

Arrange the fruits and vegetables on the material. It is o.k. if they overlap, or if some of them stick out over the side. In some places the plain material will show through. When you have found a pleasing design, glue the fruits and vegetables down. Then put the stick through the hem.

Tie a double piece of thread to each side of the stick. All you need to do now is to hang your masterpiece.

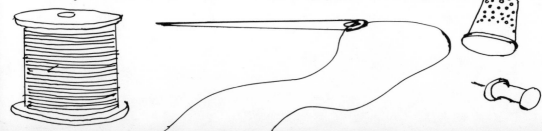

Potato Print Wrapping Paper

Nothing is duller than a raw potato. But with the potato (and a few other things), you can change plain paper into your own hand-made, one-of-a-kind wrapping paper.

WHAT YOU NEED

a large raw potato
a kitchen knife
poster paints
a plate
paper

WHAT TO DO

Cut the potato in half. Pick a simple shape to carve on the flat end of the potato. Diamonds, triangles, stars, arrows, fruits or flowers are good shapes to try. You can also make up your own shapes. Any shape is o.k.

With the tip of the knife, cut an outline of the shape on the potato about ¼-inch deep. Then, use the knife to chip away all the other parts of the potato — everything except the design. When you are finished, the potato should look something like this:

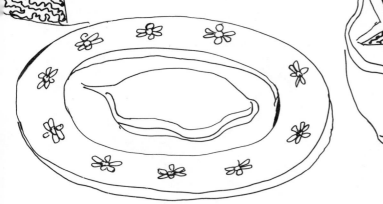

You are ready to start printing. Spread some poster paint in the middle of a plate. Dip the design into the paint until the shape is covered with paint.

Press the potato firmly on the paper. The shape you carved will now be on the paper. It may look a little uneven. Sometimes there is more paint on one part of the design than on another. But that is what makes potato print paper special.

Fill up the paper with the shape. You might want to put the shape in even rows on the paper. That way, it will have a repeat design, like wallpaper. Or try printing the design every which way.

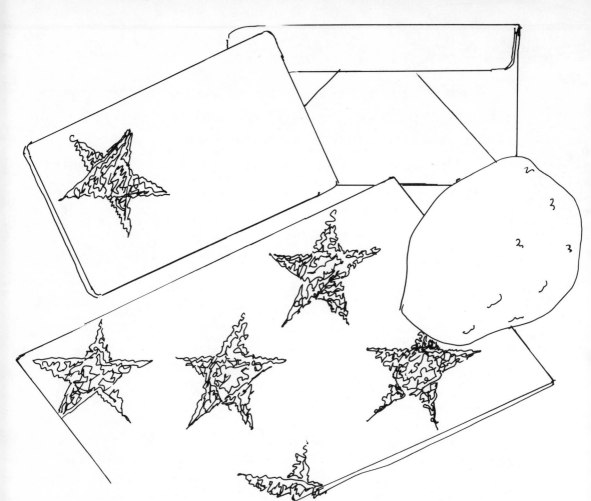

Using two colors is easy. First, put the design on the paper in one color. Then, wash the potato, dry it, and start again with another color. Try lots of combinations.

When you have finished each sheet of wrapping paper, let it dry before you use it. And don't forget to make matching cards to go with the paper. (For cards, you can use a heavier paper, such as construction paper.) Make many sheets of paper; a gift wrapped in hand-made paper is already something special.

RECIPES

Cornbread

When the Pilgrims left England, they had never seen corn. The Indians taught them how to grow and eat this American grain. Here is a recipe for a delicious, healthy bread that uses ground-up corn.

WHAT YOU NEED

1 cup whole wheat flour
1 cup corn meal
4 teaspoons baking powder
½ teaspoon salt
2 eggs
1 cup milk
¼ cup butter
4 tablespoons honey
a large mixing bowl
a square baking pan,
  or a pie pan
measuring spoons
a measuring cup
a small pan for melting
  butter
a small bowl
a fork

WHAT TO DO

Turn the oven on to 425°.

Measure 1 cup of whole wheat flour, 1 cup of corn meal, 4 teaspoons of baking powder and ½ teaspoon salt into a large mixing bowl. Stir these ingredients with a fork until they are all mixed up together.

On the stove, melt ¼ cup of butter. (The measurement is marked on the paper the butter comes in.)

Break two eggs into a small bowl. Beat them with a fork.

Add the milk to the flour mixture. Stir.

41

Then add the eggs, the melted butter and the 4 tablespoons of honey. Stir well, making sure there is no dry flour on the bottom of the bowl.

Grease the baking pan with a pat or two of butter or a large spoonful of cooking oil.

Pour the batter into the pan.

Bake for 25 minutes.

Take the pan out of the oven.

Turn the oven off.

Popcorn

You don't have to go to the movies to eat hot popcorn. The kind you make at home is fresher, it tastes better and you can have it any time you want.

WHAT YOU NEED

2 tablespoons cooking oil
½ cup popcorn (unpopped)
salt
butter
a large pot with a close-fitting lid
a spoon

43

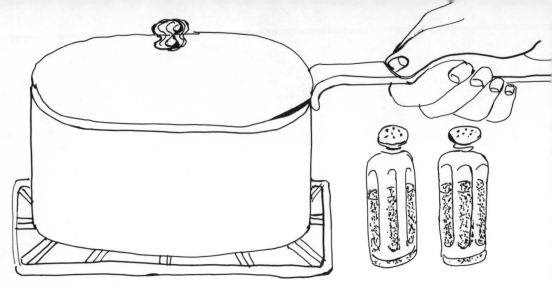

WHAT TO DO

Pour two tablespoons of cooking oil into the pot. The oil should cover the bottom of the pot. Heat for about a minute.

Pour in the popcorn. Keep the pot on the heat and at the same time, shake the popcorn around a bit. After a minute or so, you will hear the popcorn begin to pop. Keep shaking it every once in a while to make sure all the kernels pop. After another minute or two, the popping will get furious. But then it will begin to die down. When the popping has completely stopped, take the pot off the heat.

Open the lid. The pot will be filled with fresh, warm popcorn. Put it in a large bowl and it is ready to eat.

Popcorn is delicious just as it is, but some people think it is even better with a little salt and butter. Melt about 2 tablespoons of butter. Pour this over the popcorn. Sprinkle with salt. Mix it with a spoon, and serve.

Cranberry Sauce

Long before the Pilgrims even came to America, the Indians were eating cranberries. They had other names for the red berries, though. In Massachusetts and New Jersey, Indians called the berry *"ibimi,"* while in Wisconsin, they called it *"atoque."* The Pilgrims gave the cranberry its English name, but you can call it whatever you want!

WHAT YOU NEED

2 cups sugar
2 cups water
1 pound cranberries
a large pan
a mixing spoon

WHAT TO DO

Put the sugar and water in the pan. Stir over medium heat until the sugar is dissolved. This will take about 5 minutes.

Add the cranberries. Keep stirring until the cranberry skins pop.

Take the pan off the burner.

Serve the cranberry sauce warm or cold.

Winter Fruit Salad

Before people had refrigerators, fresh fruit in the winter was limited to apples stored in the cellar and an orange at Christmas. Today, we are luckier. This fresh fruit salad is tasty on Thanksgiving or any other day of the year.

WHAT YOU NEED

3 oranges
1 crisp apple
2 bananas
some fresh pineapple (or pineapple canned in its own
    juice)
1 grapefruit
a small carton of plain yogurt

a knife
a large bowl

WHAT TO DO

Cut up all the fruit into bite-size sections. Be sure to throw away the seeds, the peel and the white membrane on the orange and grapefruit. (However, you do not have to peel the apple.)

Mix the fruit in a bowl.

Serve with yogurt for a topping. For variety, add any other fresh fruits you might have on hand. Or, you can add thawed frozen berries, cut-up dates, a few raisins or a sprinkling of coconut.

This salad serves about four people.

Cherries Jamboree

For a special dessert, try plump dark cherries swimming in hot sauce and served over ice cream. You can make it in a snap.

WHAT YOU NEED

1 1-pound can of dark, sweet, pitted cherries
1 tablespoon cornstarch   a spoon
1 teaspoon honey   a pan
1 quart vanilla ice cream   a can opener

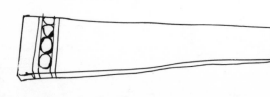

WHAT TO DO

Open the can of cherries. Pour the liquid into a pan. Heat.

Add the tablespoon of cornstarch a little at a time. Stir it up so there won't be any lumps.

Add the cherries. If you want, add a teaspoon of honey.

When the sauce is hot, take it off the heat. Scoop ice cream into bowls and spoon the hot cherry sauce over the ice cream.

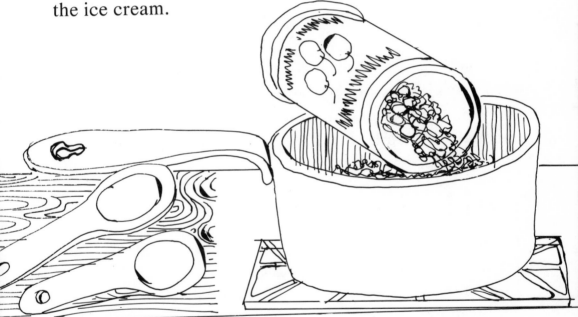

Serve. There is enough for four or five people.

This sauce is also delicious poured over angel food cake, waffles or pancakes.

Indian Pudding

Pudding didn't always come powdered from little cardboard boxes. In early America, people made a dark, spicy pudding using milk, molasses and cornmeal. You can make Indian Pudding too. It takes a long time — but the results are worth it.

WHAT YOU NEED

1 quart milk (4 cups)
1/3 cup cornmeal
1 cup molasses
3 tablespoons butter
½ teaspoon salt
½ teaspoon ginger
½ teaspoon cinnamon

2 eggs
½ cup raisins
a large pot
a spoon
a small bowl
a casserole or baking dish

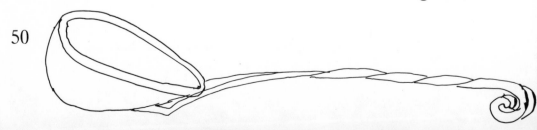

WHAT TO DO

Turn the oven to 350°.

Measure all the ingredients ahead of time.

Heat the milk until it is steamy hot. Watch the pot so the milk does not boil and spill over the sides. Gradually stir in the cornmeal. Keep stirring so it will not be lumpy.

Add molasses, butter, salt, ginger, cinnamon. Stir until thick. This will take about 15 minutes.

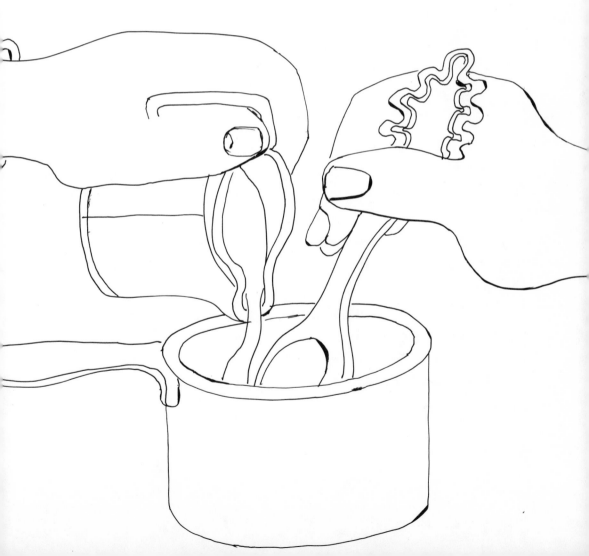

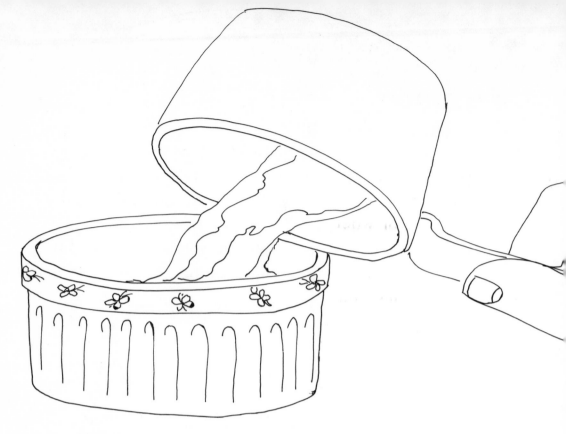

Break the eggs into a small bowl and beat with a fork or spoon. Add the beaten eggs to the mixture a little at a time. Last but not least, add the raisins. Keep stirring as you do this.

Grease the casserole with butter. Pour the mixture into it. Let it bake in the oven for 1 hour and 15 minutes. Do not stir the pudding.

When you remove the pudding from the oven, it will be bubbling. Let it sit on top of the stove for at least 20 minutes before eating.

Serve this pudding hot or cold with vanilla ice cream or regular cream.

Thanksgiving Memory Game

Sometimes, the Thanksgiving feast is not at your house but elsewhere. In that case, you may have to drive. And the trip can be long and boring. One way to pass the time in the car is to play a game. This one is easy and all you need to do is to know the alphabet and to have a good memory.

Here's how it works. Let's say you are going to spend Thanksgiving at your friend Todd's house. Each person would begin the game by saying, "We are going to Todd's house for Thanksgiving and on the table we will have..." The first person names something that begins with the letter "*a*." The next person names the thing that begins with "*a*" and then adds something beginning with "*b*." The third person names the things that begin with "*a*" and "*b*" and then adds something that begins with "*c*." And so on.

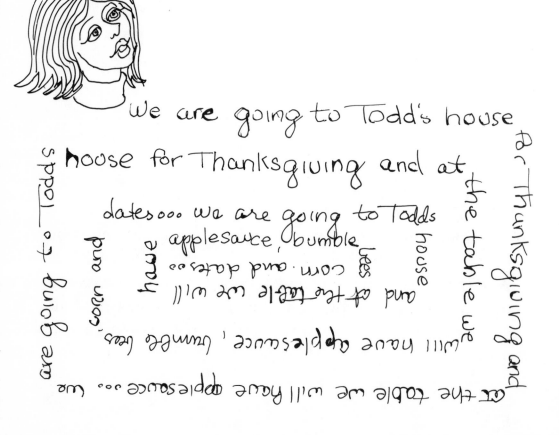

We are going to Todd's house for Thanksgiving and at the table we will have... dates... we are going to Todds house we will have applesauce, bumble bees corn and dates... we are going to Todds

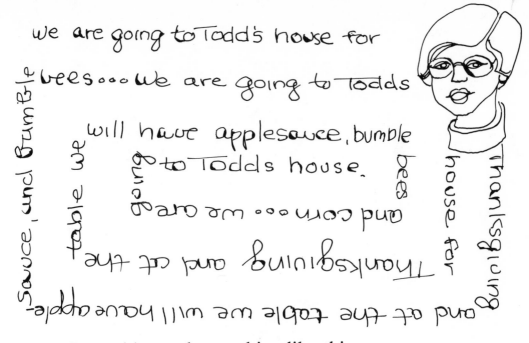

It would sound something like this:

You: We are going to Todd's house (or Grand-mother's house or wherever you are actually going) for Thanksgiving. And on the table we will have applesauce (or ants or acorns).

Next person: We are going to Todd's house for Thanksgiving and on the table we will have applesauce and bumblebees.

Third person: We are going to Todd's house for Thanksgiving and on the table we will have applesauce, bumblebees and corn.

The game gets harder and harder as you go along. See who can get the farthest without forgetting anything. Then, when you get to wherever you are going, you can tell your hosts what you *thought* they were going to have!

ABOUT THE AUTHOR

Nancy Hathaway writes fiction and articles and is the author of *Halloween Crafts and Cookbook*. She lives in Venice, California.

ABOUT THE ILLUSTRATOR

Hannah Berman is an artist and a teacher in the New York City school system. An exhibiting painter, Ms. Berman is the mother of two children and the illustrator of *Halloween Crafts and Cookbook*.